DISCARD

Masters of Music
THE WORLD'S GREATEST COMPOSERS

The Life and Times of
Duke Ellington

P.O. Box 196
Hockessin, Delaware 19707

Masters of Music
THE WORLD'S GREATEST COMPOSERS

Titles in the Series
The Life and Times of...

Johann Sebastian Bach

Ludwig van Beethoven

Irving Berlin

Hector Berlioz

Leonard Bernstein

Johannes Brahms

Frederic Chopin

Duke Ellington

Stephen Foster

W.S. Gilbert and Arthur Sullivan

George Gershwin

George Frideric Handel

Franz Joseph Haydn

Scott Joplin

Franz Liszt

Felix Mendelssohn

Wolfgang Amadeus Mozart

Franz Peter Schubert

John Philip Sousa

Igor Stravinsky

Peter Ilyich Tchaikovsky

Giuseppe Verdi

Antonio Lucio Vivaldi

Richard Wagner

Visit us on the web: www.mitchelllane.com
Comments? email us: mitchelllane@mitchelllane.com

Masters of Music
THE WORLD'S GREATEST COMPOSERS

The Life and Times of
Duke Ellington

by John Bankston

Copyright © 2005 by Mitchell Lane Publishers, Inc. All rights reserved. No part of this book may be reproduced without written permission from the publisher. Printed and bound in the United States of America.

Printing   4   5   6   7   8   9

Library of Congress Cataloging-in-Publication Data
Bankston, John, 1974-
   The Life and Times of Duke Ellington/John Bankston.
       p. cm. — (Masters of music. The world's greatest composers)
   Includes bibliographical references (p.) and index.
       ISBN 1-58415-248-6 (lib bdg.)
   1. Ellington, Duke, 1899-1974—Juvenile literature. 2. Jazz musicians—United States—Biography—Juvenile literature. [1. Ellington, Duke, 1899-1974. 2. Musicians. 3. Composers. 4. African Americans—Biography.] I. Title. II. Masters of music. World's greatest composers.
ML3930.E44B26 2004
781.65'092—dc22
                                                                              2003024123
ISBN 13: 9781584152484

ABOUT THE AUTHOR: Born in Boston, Massachussetts, **John Bankston** began publishing articles in newspapers and magazines while still a teenager. Since then, he has written over two hundred articles, and contributed chapters to books such as *Crimes of Passion,* and *Death Row 2000,* which have been sold in bookstores across the world. He has written more than three dozen biographies for young adults, including *Francis Crick and James Watson: Pioneers in DNA Research, Robert Goddard and the Liquid Rocket Engine,* and *Alexander Fleming and the Story of Penicillin* (Mitchell Lane). He has worked in Los Angeles, California as a producer, screenwriter and actor. Currently he is in pre-production on *Dancing at the Edge,* a semi-autobiographical screenplay he hopes to film in Portland, Oregon. Last year he completed his first young adult novel, *18 to Look Younger.* He currently lives in Portland, Oregon.

PHOTO CREDITS: Cover: AP Photo; pp. 6, 10, 18, 26, 32, 34, 40, 42 Hulton/Archive by Getty Images

PUBLISHER'S NOTE: This story is based on the author's extensive research, which he believes to be accurate. Documentation of such research is contained on page 46.

   The internet sites referenced herein were active as of the publication date. Due to the fleeting nature of some web sites, we cannot guarantee they will all be active when you are reading this book.

PLB4

Contents

The Life and Times of
Duke Ellington

by John Bankston

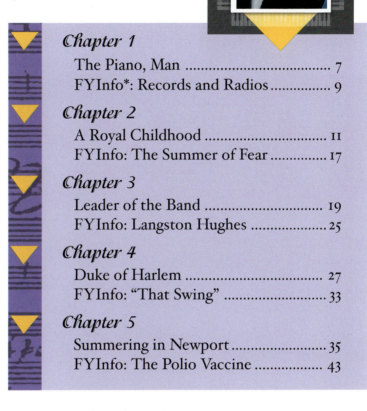

Chapter 1
The Piano, Man 7
FYInfo*: Records and Radios 9

Chapter 2
A Royal Childhood 11
FYInfo: The Summer of Fear 17

Chapter 3
Leader of the Band 19
FYInfo: Langston Hughes 25

Chapter 4
Duke of Harlem 27
FYInfo: "That Swing" 33

Chapter 5
Summering in Newport 35
FYInfo: The Polio Vaccine 43

Selected Works 44
Chronology 44
Timeline in History 45
Chapter Notes 46
Further Reading 46
Works Consulted 47
Index 48

*For Your Information

In January 1963, Duke Ellington performed at Fairfields Hall, Croydon, London. His first European tour was in 1933. Though his popularity climbed and fell over his long career, there is no doubt he is one of the most important figures in 20th century music.

Masters of Music

CHAPTER I

The Piano, Man

Inside the sweltering Philadelphia club, the 15-year-old pianist held the crowd's attention. Pounding out a ragtime rhythm, he performed with the skill and poise of someone twice his age. Already in the City of Brotherly Love he'd attracted fans. They came to tap their feet, have a good time, and try to forget the labors of the day. But in the audience that summer evening in 1914, there was one young man paying particularly close attention. He was a year younger than the musician, and his life would be forever changed by the performance.

His name was Edward Ellington. He'd traveled all the way from Asbury Park, New Jersey, just to hear Harvey Brooks play. He'd learned about Brooks from a waiter he worked with and from his uncle, a successful painter named John Kennedy, who was with Edward that night at the club.

Later Edward Ellington would explain, "I cannot tell you what that music did to me. He was swinging and he had a tremendous left hand and when I got home I had a real yearning to play. I hadn't been able to get off the ground before, but after hearing him, I said to myself, 'Man you're just going to have to do it.'"[1]

Chapter 1 - The Piano, Man

And do it he did. Just a short time after watching Brooks play, Edward caught the flu. Lying in bed, unable to do much of anything, he imagined playing as Brooks had. He could hear the notes and chords. Although he'd taken piano lessons years before, they hadn't made much of an impression.

Now he wanted to do more than play piano. He wanted to compose, to create lyrics and music. Once he felt better, he put together silly, jazzy numbers like "Poodle Dog Rag" and "What You Gonna Do When the Bed Breaks Down?"

It was the beginning of what would be a tremendous career, not just as a pianist but as a bandleader and a composer. Even as a youth, Edward Ellington had so much class and style he was given the nickname Duke. As an adult he'd also come to be known as "the Aristocrat of Swing," "the King of Swing," and "the King of Jazz." His elegance in early motion pictures not only earned him more fans and accolades but also altered many audiences' images of African Americans altogether.

More than any other musician in the early 20th century, Duke Ellington brought jazz into the nightclubs and later into the living rooms of America. The music he played sprang in part from the blues and gospel rhythms of plantation slaves living in the middle 19th century, infused with the sounds of ragtime from the turn of the century. Jazz has been called the first musical form created in the United States. It was a type of sharp improvisation for which band members played anything they wanted along a chosen key or set of chords, so every night the music was different. Duke led with his piano playing, but he allowed the various other members of his band to shine, too.

Embracing new technologies like radio receivers and record players, Duke Ellington was one of the first pop stars. ◆

FYInfo

Records and Radios

Guglielmo Marconi

Although both record players and radio receivers existed in some fashion well before Duke Ellington was born, they didn't become widely available to consumers until he was beginning his musical career.

Invented by Thomas Edison in 1877, the first "records" were tin tubes that recorded sound vibrations along a groove; when a stylus or needle was inserted into the groove and the cylinder revolved, it was possible to hear the recording. Edison's first recording was "Mary Had a Little Lamb."

Flat records would be invented 10 years later by Emile Berliner, but it wasn't until 1915 that the standard 78-rpm (revolutions per minute) phonograph album was distributed. Since the records held less than four minutes of music per side, musicians often had to shorten their works to fit. In 1948, long-playing or LP records, which ran at 33 rpm, were invented by Columbia Records.

Radio waves were first "harnessed" by Guglielmo Marconi a few years before Duke Ellington's birth. After building his first transmitter and receiver in 1895, in 1901 Marconi was able to send signals across the English Channel. Although radio became a preferred method of communicating with ships at sea, its cost made it unaffordable for most families. And besides, what would they listen to? There weren't any radio stations.

That changed in the 1920s as improved technology made radios cheaper and stations blossomed to fill the increasing demand.

The incredible growth in both record sales and radio technology happened at the beginning of Ellington's career, and he did everything he could to take advantage of it.

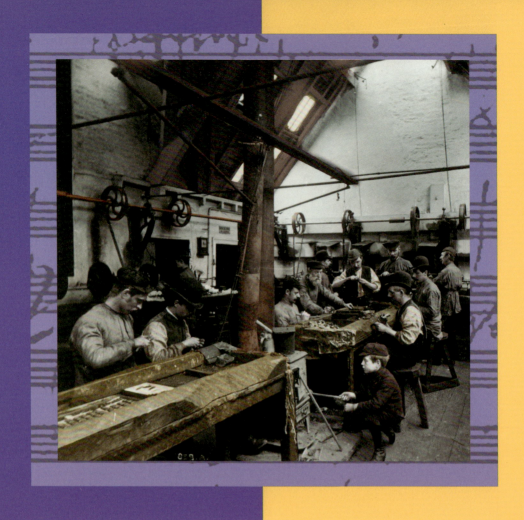

Millions of immigrants arrived in the United States in the late 1890s. The industrial revolution provided work in production plants across the nation. This photograph shows immigrants working in a metal shop in 1899.

CHAPTER 2

A Royal Childhood

It was the fin de siècle, the end of the century, a time of sophistication and artistic achievement. The 1890s began with economic collapse and the worst depression the country had yet seen. Millions lost their jobs and businesses as railroad stocks plunged, taking much of the stock market's value with them.

By 1899, a mood of restless excitement took hold. The 20th century seemed to promise prosperity, with "modern" inventions improving the lives of average citizens. Already such gadgetry as telephones and indoor plumbing was changing the way many Americans lived. The country was once primarily rural, given over to farmland and agriculture. With the industrial revolution's factories came the growth of cities as immigrants from across the world arrived to work in production plants. Meanwhile improved farming techniques required fewer people to work to feed the many.

Yet entertainment was as it had been for a hundred years. The phonograph and motion pictures were brand-new Thomas Edison inventions—for most families entertainment came from the piano in their living room. Nearly everybody had one. And just like today where people wait for the latest, hottest CD releases, in 1899

Chapter 2 - A Royal Childhood

people waited for the newest sheet music. The pages of notes and chords made stars out of composers like John Philip Sousa and Scott Joplin. A kid growing up at the turn of the last century might have idolized these music writers, just as many kids today look up to platinum-selling pop stars.

Yet while for many Americans the end of the 19th century was a time of hope and excitement, for African Americans it was a time of uncertainty and fear. Following the Civil War's conclusion in 1865, the victorious North sent soldiers south to enforce the newly granted rights of African Americans. Suddenly men who had been slaves could vote, even hold elected office. But this period of Reconstruction was short-lived, and when troops left the South in the 1870s, the new freedoms largely disappeared. In 1896, the Supreme Court decision in *Plessy v. Ferguson* legalized racial segregation in public places, saying separate but equal facilities were constitutionally acceptable. Because of this decision, many African Americans, especially in the South, rarely attended the same schools as whites. In some instances they couldn't sit at the same counter or even use the same drinking fountain.

When Edward Kennedy Ellington was born on April 29, 1899, his rights as an American, even his safety, would always be in doubt. His birthplace, Washington, D.C., was a city divided. It owned a Southern heritage and attitude: It served not just as the United States capital, but had also been the Union capital during the Civil War. Edward's life would be similarly divided. He'd often perform for white audiences but endured prejudice because of his skin color.

The challenges he faced didn't make him less bold. Some Americans might have considered him a second-class citizen because of his race, but as far as Edward was concerned, he was first-class all the way. It was a self-confidence he had his parents to thank for.

Edward's mother, Daisy Kennedy Ellington, grew up in a tight-knit, middle-class home where her father was a police captain—a very rare position for an African American in the 1800s. Rarer still, Daisy graduated from high school.

Her husband, James Edward Ellington, whom everyone called J.E., had dropped out of school in the eighth grade, yet he came across as well educated and well bred. His poise enabled him to earn a position working as a butler for a wealthy white doctor named F. Cuthbert. Inside the doctor's mansion on 1462 Rhode Island Avenue Northwest, J.E. did everything from overseeing the cook and cleaning staff to assisting with scheduling and organizing various functions. It was a very responsible and respected job, and J.E. was well suited for it.

Although the Ellingtons weren't rich, J.E. made sure the family lived as if they were. There was steak on the table and new clothes in his closet. Everything in the house had to be the best.

As much as his father took care of him, Edward's mother spoiled him. She had lost a child in infancy, so she was very protective of Edward. When Edward was suffering through a childhood bout with pneumonia, she refused to leave her son's side, sleeping in his room and making sure he was always comfortable. "You are blessed," she often told her son, and he believed it.[1]

Edward embraced his parents' values, believing as they did in the importance of good manners and proper social etiquette. His young female cousins recalled how even as a child Edward demanded a curtsy from them, and although they resented it, something about him made it impossible to refuse.

Only one thing in the Ellington household was nearly as important as good manners and social graces: music.

Chapter 2 - A Royal Childhood

Like most middle-class families, the Ellingtons had a piano. Although J.E. didn't read music, he could play opera selections by ear. Daisy did read music and frequently performed a range of songs, from popular pieces and classical compositions to selections from the 19th Street Baptist Church (J.E. attended the John Wesley A.M.E. Zion—most Sundays Edward went to church twice.) Edward once told an interviewer his earliest memory was hearing his mother playing "The Rosary." It was so beautiful, he said, "I bust out crying."[2]

Despite his parents' musical tendencies, Edward had little use for the piano. Like most kids of the time, he endured his share of piano lessons. For Edward, being outside on a baseball diamond or watching the Washington Senators play was infinitely more exciting than being cooped up with a piano.

When Edward turned five, Daisy lied and said he was six. Soon he was in first grade at Garnet Elementary School. He'd discovered a creative outlet he preferred to music: drawing. For him art class was just about the only class worth his time. His grades were mediocre, not because he wasn't bright, but because he felt the same way about school lessons as he did about piano lessons—they were an awful excuse to be indoors.

His free time he spent at Griffith Stadium, where the Senators played Major League Baseball. The only way he could watch the game was by applying for a job at the park. "I succeeded in getting one and had my first experience of stage fright," he admitted in his memoir, *Music Is My Mistress*. "I had to walk around, in and out in front of all those people, yelling, 'Peanuts, popcorn, chewing gum, candy, cigars, cigarettes and score cards!' I soon got over my nervousness, although the first day I missed a lot of the game hiding behind the stands."[3]

Edward avoided getting in too much trouble as a kid, but that was probably more by luck than by anything else. He wasn't afraid to take chances, and while that was a great asset for a musician, for a teenager it kept him just one step away from being suspended at school or in trouble at home.

By the time he was 12 years old, he'd figured out how to sneak into the Gayety Theater, a burlesque house featuring musical acts, comedy, and numerous scantily clad dancing women. Watching them, he appreciated their beauty and their performances, but he also began to wonder about performing for a living. He realized he'd like to earn a living onstage, he just wasn't sure how.

When he wasn't sneaking into the Gayety Theater, he was sneaking into the pool hall, earning extra cash competing against the best players. Being a pool hustler wasn't a great career, but it gave him the chance to mingle with adults from different walks of life. Edward's comfort with people whose careers ranged from driving buses to performing surgery would serve him well.

In 1913, Edward entered the Armstrong Manual Training School, hoping to study commercial art. There were better schools nearby, and Armstrong Manual had a reputation for attracting some pretty rough kids. However, by then Edward had decided that commercial art would feed his creative needs and provide him with a decent career.

Edward stood out from the other kids: He was better spoken and a sharper dresser. His friend Edward McEntree noticed this, giving him the name he'd be known by for the rest of his life: Duke.

In the summer of 1914, Duke was working as a dishwasher when a waiter named Bowser invited him to come hear Harvey Brooks play. Duke had already heard of Brooks from his uncle John, and he

Chapter 2 - A Royal Childhood

didn't need much arm-twisting to agree to a trip to Philadelphia. Watching the ragtime pianist play changed Duke's life.

Ragtime was exciting. Its chord changes were nothing like those in the classical compositions he'd been forced to practice as a kid. Just as important, Brooks had fans and girlfriends, and everything about the piano player's life seemed more exciting than that of a commercial artist. And it sure beat washing dishes.

Duke returned to playing the piano. This time he didn't bother with reading music, with figuring out chords and notes. Instead he banged away on the instrument, playing the songs that were in his head, trying to make them come out the way he imagined them. It was hard work, but he was good at it. Somehow he'd inherited his father's gift for playing by ear.

The year after he heard Brooks play, Duke's only sibling, Ruth, was born. Perhaps with a new baby in the house, his parents had less time to worry about him. He made the most of his freedom.

Besides the songs he made up, Duke improvised the popular music he was listening to—jazzing it up. By the time he was in his middle teens he was sharp enough to get paying jobs at small clubs and for senior parties. Just as he'd noticed with Brooks, the girls seemed to love piano players.

It was a dream come true.

Still, he had a tough decision to make. He'd entered an art contest sponsored by the National Association for the Advancement of Colored People (NAACP) and won a full scholarship to New York City's Pratt Institute. It could be the opportunity of a lifetime—but it wasn't to be the opportunity of Duke's lifetime. He turned the scholarship down. Instead, by February 1917, he'd dropped out of high school and embarked on the unconventional life of a professional musician.

The Summer of Fear

FYInfo

In the spring of 1919, Private William Little of Georgia returned to the country he'd risked his life to defend. Arriving at the tiny train station in Blakeley, he wore the only clothes he owned: the uniform of a United States soldier.

Little was greeted at the station by a group of white men who demanded that the African American remove his uniform and walk home in his underwear. He refused, and escaped only because a few other whites protected him. Little continued to wear his uniform, and soon letters arrived at his home threatening his life. He refused to give in. He'd already risked his life during the war in Europe; he wasn't afraid of risking it for a cause more personal and specific. On April 3, Little's body was discovered. He'd been beaten to death.

Carl Sandburg

In July the same year, an African-American boy swam across an invisible line into the white area of a Chicago beach. Some of the men there picked up rocks, throwing them at the boy until he was knocked unconscious. The boy drowned. Police refused to charge anyone with the murder.

Racial tension exploded in the summer of 1919 for a number of reasons, including the return of African-American soldiers who began to demand the same rights as white citizens—rights they'd risked their lives to protect. In the South the destructive boll weevil insect devastated the cotton crop, sparking a migration of poor Southern farmers, both black and white. Their qualifications might have been equal, but many of the whites demanded first access to jobs and housing in the North.

Riots plagued at least 19 cities that summer. Across the South some 76 African Americans were lynched—hung by mobs who accused them of "crimes" like looking at a white woman or lingering in a white neighborhood.

In Ellington's hometown of Washington, D.C., a riot was halted by armed white soldiers and sailors. According to some accounts, the military men badly beat a number of black rioters while allowing the whites to leave in peace.

Writer Carl Sandburg's newspaper accounts of that summer were later put into book form, called *The Chicago Race Riots,* but despite the reporting of Sandburg and numerous other writers, the problem persisted. Similar riots and racially based murders continued to take place, particularly during the civil rights conflicts of the 1960s.

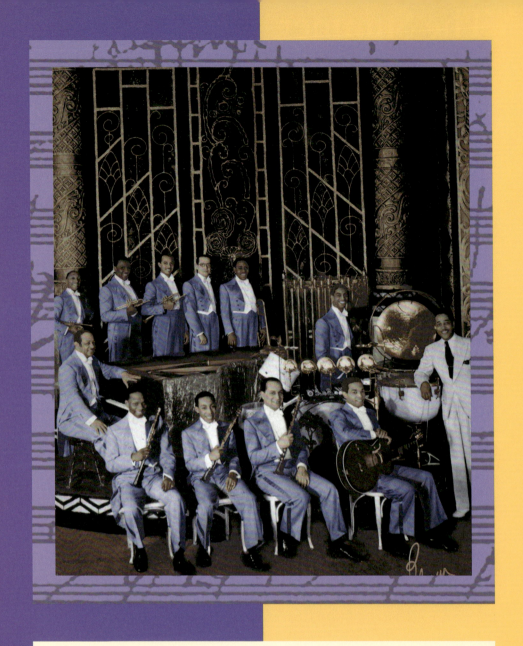

Duke Ellington (right) poses with his orchestra on stage at the Regal Theatre in Chicago, Illinois. From left to right: Freddy Jenkins, Wellman Braud, Cootie Williams, Harry Carney, Juan Tizol, Johnny Hodges, Tricky Sam Nanton, Barney Bigard, Sonny Greer, Fred Guy, and Duke.

Masters of Music

CHAPTER 3

Leader of the Band

As Edward "Duke" Ellington began an uncertain career as a professional musician, much of the world was facing a different kind of uncertainty. It began when Archduke Ferdinand, the heir to the Austrian throne, and his wife were assassinated in Sarajevo, Serbia, on June 28, 1914. In the United States the shooting was barely noticed, but it began a war that would cost millions of lives. Suspecting that the assassin was supported by Serbia, Austria made demands that provoked the other country. Unsatisfied with the Serbian response, Austria declared war. Austria's ally Germany pledged its support, while Serbian ally Russia quickly sent troops to the Russia-Austria border.

Thus began the conflict that at first was known as the Great War; eventually it would be called World War I. Before it ended, most of Europe, along with Canada and the United States, was involved.

By 1917 the United States had joined the war effort and thousands of young Americans were boarding ships bound for Europe. Over 100,000 would not return. Duke Ellington was fortunate, as he was able to stay in the country working as a messenger for the Navy and then the State Department. For a musician working in

Chapter 3 - Leader of the Band

Washington, D.C., the war had an unexpected benefit, because events honoring important people, from military officers to foreign dignitaries, increased dramatically. At every one of those events, a piano player was needed. So while Duke's parents might have worried about their son leaving high school to become a musician, Duke was able to work as much as he wanted to.

Just a year after leaving high school, he formed a band—The Duke's Serenaders. The band featured Duke on piano, a drummer, a saxophonist, and a guitar or banjo. Their first gig was just two blocks from Duke's home, at the True Reformer's Hall.

Inside Room 10 at Seventh and T Streets Northwest, Duke Ellington made his first money as a bandleader. Performing on what he claimed was "the worst piano in the world," he played from 8:00 P.M. to 1:00 A.M. for three shiny quarters. "Man I snatched that money and ran like a thief," he later recalled for the *Washington Star*. "My mother was so proud of me."[1]

He gave her plenty of reason to be proud. Soon Duke was living on his own, with a telephone (two years before his parents had one) and an ad in the phone book advertising "Irresistable Jass." It turns out Duke was more than just a great piano player and composer. He was a top-notch businessman as well.

Clients noticed how whenever they called Duke about a job, he always seemed in a rush—like someone who had more work than he could handle. This made them want to hire him even more. Of course, sometimes he wasn't busy. He just realized that speaking quickly and seeming hurried was the best way to appear successful.

Before too long the man everyone called Duke was performing before the capital's aristocracy, entertaining politicians and others in high society. As his professional life blossomed, his personal life also changed. Shortly before he left high school, he met Edna

Thompson. By the time they were married on July 2, 1918, he was successful enough to afford a new house and car. The following spring they had a son, Mercer. Born on March 11, he would be their only child—their second died in infancy. During this time, Duke did more than just play music. Even the most talented entertainers understand when they are starting out that they need a reliable source of money to fall back on—a day job. This is why most actors are also waiters. Duke put his talents as an artist to work; he painted signs, a job he could do when work as a musician wasn't steady.

Writer F. Scott Fitzgerald called the 1920s "the jazz age," and as a musician Duke Ellington was one of the best representatives of the decade. By the time the tragic conflict of World War I ended with Germany signing a peace treaty on November 11, 1918, the United States was ready to celebrate.

Musicians were employed in greater numbers than ever before, and by the early 1920s, Duke Ellington and the Serenaders definitely had more work than they could handle. They also began working in bars and nightclubs, which had once been legal but became illegal when Congress passed the law of Prohibition.

Beginning in 1920, Prohibition made the manufacture or sale of alcohol illegal, so many of the places Duke played were operating against the law. Protecting themselves by requiring patrons to use a secret knock or a password to get admitted, these clubs were called "speakeasies." Many served a homemade alcohol called "bathtub gin" or relied on black market alcohol supplied by bootleggers smuggling it in from Canada.

Prohibition sparked an increase in crime and made it tough to be a drinker, but it was a great time to play jazz. Nearly every speakeasy from small to large needed musicians, and while Duke

Chapter 3 - Leader of the Band

had played at high-class parties during WWI, performing in seedier establishments had its own reward.

The money improved, for one thing, and Duke was able to focus entirely on his playing, leaving the sign-painting business behind. Unfortunately there were risks as well. Cornet player Rex Stewart remembered in an interview, "Once the police shot it out with bootleggers. . . . Ambulances were rarely seen in a coloured neighborhood in those days and the victim generally bled to death."[2]

Although he was the bandleader of a successful musical act, Duke was pulled in several different directions. He had to deal with the tension that resulted from being a musician at night, with its temptations to drink after work and opportunities to meet many women, and being a family man during the day.

Just as challenging, Duke's band was getting restless. Washington, D.C., was a small town compared to jazz's epicenter. Any jazz player who thought he was talented wanted to test his chops in the most competitive place in the country: New York City. In the 1920s, jazz was a big part of Harlem, an area 25 blocks long and 6 blocks wide in New York's Manhattan. African-American artists of all types lived and worked in Harlem. The Harlem Renaissance of the 1920s was mostly described by writers like Langston Hughes, so today it is often viewed as a literary movement. However, in its heyday it was powered by all types of creative people.

If New York City's Harlem was jazz's solar system, then the Cotton Club was its sun, the one body around which everything else spun, the one place with a strong enough pull to attract players who are still known generations later. One of those musicians is Cab Calloway, who in his autobiography, *Of Minnie the Moocher and Me*, describes the club that opened in 1923 and could hold 700 customers as "a huge room. The bandstand was a replica of a Southern mansion, with large white columns and a backdrop painted with weeping willows and slave quarters. The band played on the veranda of the mansion and in front of the veranda, down a few steps, was the dance floor which was also used for shows. The waiters were dressed in red tuxedos, like butlers in a Southern mansion . . . and there were huge crystal cut chandeliers."[3]

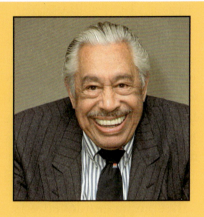

Cab Calloway was another popular bandleader of the 1930s who was known for his rhythmic refrain, "hi-de-hi-de-ho." Here he is shown later in life.

The club, which was on 142nd Street, was also all white. Black entertainers performed there, but African Americans weren't allowed as customers. It was the type of segregation Duke Ellington would encounter for much of his career.

In 10 years the African-American population of Harlem would more than double, reaching 165,000 by 1930. The Serenaders were ready to join the northern migration by 1923, but Duke was reluctant. After all, they had a good thing in Washington, D.C, a steady income and a growing reputation. He had a family to support; he wasn't about to pull up roots for a gamble.

In the winter of 1923, Wilbur Sweatman made the band an offer Duke couldn't refuse. Sweatman needed a new drummer for his band. He sent a telegraph to William "Sonny" Greer asking if he was interested in the job. Greer replied that he'd accept only if he

Chapter 3 - Conflict

could bring his bandmates, with Duke on piano and Otto Hardwick on sax. Sweatman agreed.

Even with guaranteed employment, Duke wasn't sure, but a month before his 24th birthday he decided to risk it. Arriving in New York City, he was unprepared for how difficult working for someone else would be.

Duke was used to being the leader. Suddenly he was sharing a vaudeville stage at the Lafayette Theatre with Sweatman, who did a musical comedy act and relied on the musicians to back him up. When their weeklong gig ended, Sweatman expected Duke and his players to follow him on a multicity tour of the United States. Duke had another idea. He got together with Greer and Hardwick and asked them to make a choice: follow Sweatman, or take a risk finding work in New York. They decided to stay.

Becoming employed was nearly impossible. They didn't have the reputation they'd had in D.C.; instead they were unknowns competing against some of the best in their business. The group quickly ran out of money. The only money they made was from rent parties.

Huge numbers of people flowing into Harlem drove up rental prices. In order to make ends meet, whenever someone couldn't afford rent, they threw a party. Charging a cover and selling liquor, they usually collected enough for another month. Entertainment was usually provided by a band or a piano player. Duke and his band never made more than a couple of bucks at these gigs.

Still, after a few months without steady work, the Serenaders were desperate. When Duke found 15 dollars lying on the street, he took it as some sort of sign. He bought the band a last good meal in Harlem and train tickets back to D.C. As far as Duke Ellington was concerned, the Harlem music scene could make it without him. ◆

Langston Hughes: The Renaissance Reporter

FYInfo

"Hold fast to dreams, for if dreams die, life is a broken winged bird that cannot fly."—Langston Hughes

The Harlem Renaissance of the 1920s was sparked by a combination of African-American migration to Harlem and many people's hunger for the music and literature of the African-American community. In Harlem nightclubs, white audiences cheered African-American jazz and blues players, while other whites financially supported African-American writers like Zora Neale Hurston and Alain Locke.

Langston Hughes

Among the writers who emerged from the 1920s Harlem Renaissance, few are as well known and well respected as Langston Hughes.

Hughes moved to Harlem around the same time as Duke Ellington, having dropped out of Columbia University to pursue a writing career. Working at a series of odd jobs before landing his first book contract, he was promoted by writer Carl Van Vechten and poet Vachel Lindsay as the "busboy poet."

Hughes became the second African American to earn a living as a writer, following his idol Paul Laurence Dunbar. Hughes's work—novels, poems, plays, and even newspaper columns—would illustrate not only his own personal struggles but the struggles of human beings everywhere. His ability to transcend race helped make him popular with all audiences. His struggle to succeed in a country scarred by racial prejudice and segregation affected anyone who had overcome obstacles while pursuing his or her dreams.

Traveling widely, Hughes enjoyed the freedom of appearing Mexican in Mexico (he spoke fluent Spanish) and interacting with many white tourists who might not have given him the day's time had they known he was African American. Going to the Soviet Union, he embraced communism, impressed by a political system that seemed to be without segregation, providing jobs and health care for everyone regardless of their background. Only years later would he renounce the system as he realized that communism's ideals and its realities were far different—especially when practiced under Soviet dictator Joseph Stalin.

In many ways, Hughes's greatest achievement was defining the Harlem Renaissance while not being defined by it. His career continued successfully until his death in 1967.

This publicity picture of Duke was taken around 1940. Duke remained a powerful performer well into his sixties and seventies.

Masters of Music

CHAPTER 4

Duke of Harlem

When Duke Ellington returned to his wife and son at their house in the nation's capital, it was a bitter sweet homecoming. He'd wanted to conquer New York's jazz scene. Instead he'd come back with little more than pocket change. He quickly found work as a pianist and began paying the bills he'd let pile up during his New York adventure.

Although he might have thought his trip north was the last time he'd be in New York, it wasn't. In June another chance came along, and Duke seized it. Greer told him there was a job waiting in Harlem. Duke bought a first-class ticket, put on his best suit, and made his way to New York to find that the job no longer existed.

It would be a long, hot summer.

The band spent the season traveling by overheated subway car from audition to fruitless audition. Looking for a new source of income, Duke teamed up with Jo Trent and began writing songs, hoping to sell them to a publisher. In the beginning he had the same luck with this as he did finding a gig: none at all. He kept trying, and by summer's end, Duke even tackled radio.

Chapter 4 - Duke of Harlem

Although radio had been around for decades, it didn't become a popular form of entertainment for the average person until the 1920s, when radio receivers became affordable. Even then there weren't many stations. When Duke performed with a blues musician on an August broadcast, he didn't attract too many listeners.

During their early time in New York, Duke wasn't the band's leader. Instead that job went to a man named Elmer Snowden, who helped them find work in Atlantic City, New Jersey, and even put Duke on his first record, playing with his band the Novelty Orchestra. Snowden ran the band until the next year, when the rest of the members kicked him out for taking too much of the money. After that, Duke returned to his previous job as bandleader —a position he'd hold for the next 50 years.

In September 1923, things improved when Snowden helped Duke and the rest of the band land a gig playing at the Hollywood Club, signing a contract to be the house band until the following March. Although the club wasn't in Harlem, the band needed the money. Located near Times Square, a fairly dangerous entertainment district in mid-Manhattan, the Hollywood Club on 49th Street was dark and cramped, especially when it reached a capacity of just over one hundred people—far less than what the Cotton Club could hold.

Maybe it wasn't uptown, but the location guaranteed them publicity. Soon Duke was leading a regular spot every Wednesday afternoon on radio station WHN's 3:15 broadcast. Despite having few listeners, by getting comfortable with the new medium, Duke was preparing for bigger and better things. In just a few years, there would be more people listening to the radio than going to the movies.

By the time the band began playing at the Hollywood, they had a new name as well, the Washingtonians, in honor of their hometown. The band began getting press attention. In the *Clipper,* a trade magazine for the entertainment industry, writer Abel Green said, "The boys can seemingly satisfy without exerting themselves, but for the benefit of the *Clipper* reviewer they brought out a variety of instruments upon which each demonstrated his versatility. And how!"[1] They gained such an audience of devoted listeners that the Hollywood Club offered to extend the band's contract. Duke Ellington and the Washingtonians would play there for over three years.

Duke refused to relax. Along with collaborator Jo Trent, Duke continued to try to sell songs. In 1923, the pair copyrighted "Blind Man's Bluff," but it didn't sell.

Inside the Hollywood Club, every night after the band's regular ten, midnight, and two A.M. slots, Duke would wheel his piano onto the floor. Approaching couples, he'd ask the gentleman at the table if he wanted a song played for his lady. The men rarely refused—most of the people in the club were doing well, flush with cash from the stock market or bootlegging. Duke often made more from tips than he earned playing.

Easy money had a price.

In 1926 the Hollywood Club (renamed Club Kentucky) ran into trouble with the law for selling liquor. With their regular gig padlocked, the band again hit the streets to find work.

This time it was easier.

As summer's scorching heat approached, they signed with tour promoter Charles Shribman. He booked them in the cooler towns of New England, often double-billing them with an all-white band. Duke Ellington and the Washingtonians spent the summer of 1926 performing from Rhode Island to Maine.

Chapter 4 - Duke of Harlem

When fall rolled around, Club Kentucky was back in business and the band was back on stage. Besides his time as a bandleader, Duke was exploring another moneymaker: records. Although he'd done one recording with Snowden and a second with his band for the Victor label, it wasn't until 1924 that his recording career went into high gear as he released seven different 78s. Since they held less than four minutes of music per side and had poor sound quality, Duke tailored his work to fit them.

Outside the recording studio and the radio station booth, Duke's career continued to blossom. In 1926, one man, Irving Mills, was responsible for getting Duke a few higher-paying bookings. Both as manager and the owner of a record label, Mills was a white man happy to work with the predominantly African-American jazz musicians he signed and promoted. The agreement between Duke and Mills gave each man 45 percent of the company Duke formed, with the extra 10 percent going to their lawyer. Since Mills had an enormous financial interest in Duke's career, he tirelessly promoted the young bandleader.

Irving Mills was Duke's personal manager from 1927 to 1939.

By 1927, Duke and the Washingtonians were ready for a move uptown. They were ready for the Cotton Club. The death of house bandleader Andy Preer left an opening at the club. Duke took it.

In two years, from 1927 to 1929, the number of radios in American households nearly tripled, and playing at the Cotton Club gave the band a unique opportunity to be heard. The club had a microphone connected to a radio station. Besides broadcasting their regular late-night performances, the band occasionally performed during the dinner hour, when, as Sonny Greer boasted in an interview, "Everybody was waiting for that from New York to California. . . . Of course you know that's supportive. All the people didn't get anybody anything to eat until we come off. Cats working all day, starved to death until we get off."[2]

Duke seemed a natural on these programs, but he'd been working hard for years to seem so relaxed on the air.

The radio business of the 1920s resembled the Internet business of the 1990s. Many Americans believed that radio stations would continue to be built in huge numbers for years and years. It seemed as if everyone was an investor in radio stocks, purchasing shares in fledgling companies that promised huge returns. Many of these investors bought on margin, paying just 10 percent of the stock's cost and betting they could pay back the loan when the stock price increased. If the stock fell, not only would they lose their investment, but they would also be required to pay back the loan.

Most investors were unprepared for their radio stocks to drop in value. They were blindsided by what happened next.

In 1929, the stock market didn't just drop, it crashed. It would take nearly 20 years for the market to regain what it lost that year. In the meantime many companies, including radio companies, went

Chapter 4 - Duke of Harlem

out of business, just as so many Internet companies failed in the late 1990s.

Soon one out of four Americans who wanted a job couldn't find one. Many Americans became homeless. Duke and the Washingtonians would soon find themselves playing for less money, but it wasn't the Great Depression that hurt the band. It was a new style of music, and the worst part was that Duke would give it its name.

Workers flood the streets on Wall Street, New York City in a panic following the stock market crash on October 29, 1929. Soon after, nearly one out of four Americans were unemployed and many ended up homeless.

"THAT SWING" FYInfo

"It Ain't Got a Thing (If It Ain't Got That Swing)" was more than a song written by Duke Ellington. In many ways it seemed like a prediction.

In 1926, New York's Savoy Ballroom had opened with a block-long dance floor and a double-decker bandstand. The club quickly became packed with some of the most skilled dancers in the city. The following year many of them would be doing steps named after a headline. Reporting on aviator Charles Lindbergh's record-setting transoceanic flight, one paper proclaimed, "Lindy Hops the Atlantic."

Louis Armstrong

Soon the Lindy Hop and its variation, the jitterbug, were being practiced by young adults across the country. Featuring high-spirited steps, the bigger dances seemed to cry out for bigger bands.

Although Ellington popularized the term *swing* and African-American musicians such as Louis Armstrong first played it, white dance fans seemed to prefer white dance bands, like the one led by Benny Goodman.

Author Stanley Dance noted, "The general preference of white masses for jazz musicians was never altogether the result of racial prejudice. Translations and indeed dilutions were understandably more to their taste."[3] This "taste" severely crimped the ability of jazz bands like Ellington's to make a living.

Swing peaked in the 1940s with the return of sailors and soldiers who'd fought in World War II. Soon it evolved into regional styles like West Coast Swing and the Whip of Houston, Texas.

In the late 1990s, bands like the Brian Setzer Orchestra and the Daddies briefly repopularized the style.

Charles Lindbergh

This is a group portrait of Duke and his band taken in 1934, at the height of his popularity. They are pictured in Los Angeles, California. Ivie Anderson is pictured to the left of Duke.

Masters of Music

CHAPTER 5

Summering in Newport

The jazz age, the 1920s, was a free-spirited time with its own free-spirited sound track. The booming stock market and illegal bootleg dollars put money in the pockets of millionaires and the people who drove their cars. The stock market crash and Prohibition's repeal changed everything.

Speakeasies were hit with a double whammy. The Great Depression of the 1930s left few people with the money for extras like entertainment, and alcohol's re-legalization removed the very reason for speakeasies to exist.

Musicians were hard hit as the jobs dried up. Those that continued to work, like Duke Ellington and the Washingtonians, had built reputations that would withstand the bad times. Still, the band and its leader faced challenges. Although it was never as difficult as it had been in the early jobless days when they'd first arrived in New York, they had to scramble to find gigs. Irving Mills continued to release Duke's records, although fewer people were spending money on them.

Radio was huge. Over one third of American households owned a receiver, and tuning in a station was cheaper than buying albums

Chapter 5 - Summering in Newport

or going to clubs. Duke and the Washingtonians became a regular presence on numerous radio programs.

By then they'd also moved into another forum: movies.

Until 1927, movies didn't have much use for bands. Before then they were silent. Any words the actors said were displayed on title cards, and compositions were played by a live musician inside the individual movie theaters. *The Jazz Singer* changed everything. Released in 1927, it was the first "talkie" from a major studio. Besides audible dialogue, it had built-in music. After that, movie bands were in great demand.

Duke Ellington did more than just make money.

African-American movie actors usually played stereotypical roles. They played servants and spoke in exaggerated dialects. Not Duke. On screen he was the same well-spoken, sharply dressed musician that he was in real life. As respected as he'd been as a composer, he gained even greater respect within the African-American community by refusing to allow himself to be degraded by stereotyping.

As the band's success grew, Duke's own life seemed to be falling apart. In 1929 his marriage ended, and he moved into an apartment with his girlfriend on Sugar Hill, an upscale area of Harlem. He brought his parents and his sister up from Washington, D.C., and moved them in with him.

In 1931 the band ended their time at the Cotton Club and began to tour the country. Irving Mills pressed Duke to tour the South, where there was a great deal of money to be made. Duke was reluctant. He knew how segregated the region was, and when he finally agreed many of his worries came true. There were no hotels that would accept African Americans, so they had to stay in broken-down boardinghouses or private homes. The "dressing room" was usually a janitor's closet.

The next time they toured, Duke came up with an ingenious solution. The band rented a pair of well-appointed private railroad cars. The cars could be unhitched at their destination, serving as dressing room and hotel. It was, Duke liked to point out, the way the President traveled.

After his marriage, Duke faced more losses. In 1935 his mother died, and he sank into a deep depression. His record output slowed, and he canceled performances.

Although the decline in Duke's fortunes was partly related to the loss of his mother, it was also connected to the changing tastes of the American public. For over a decade they'd embraced jazz, and now they were ready to swing. Duke himself had popularized the word with the song "It Ain't Got a Thing (If It Ain't Got That Swing)," but by the middle 1930s, swing bands led by men like Jimmy Dorsey and Benny Goodman were eclipsing bands like the Washingtonians. Although Duke and his band were accomplished in a form of swing jazz, they weren't an actual swing band.

In 1937, after years of battling alcoholism, Duke's father, J.E. Ellington, succumbed to the disease. Besides the personal sadness of losing both his parents before he was 40, Duke struggled to pay the enormous medical bills his parents had run up prior to their deaths. He took advances on his earnings from Mills and several others—advances that would take years to pay off.

In order to make enough money, Duke Ellington and the Washingtonians left the United States. They'd toured Europe before, happily performing in Paris and London, places where the audiences were appreciative and racial prejudices were not as profound

Chapter 5 - Summering in Newport

Jimmy Dorsey (left) and Benny Goodman. An increasing number of white musicians played big band jazz in the 1930s. Clarinetist Benny Goodman popularized "swing."

as they were in the States. However, the European tour of 1939 faced unique obstacles. In England a dispute with the musicians union kept the band from playing at all. The rest of the continent, watching the rise of Adolf Hitler, faced the threat of war.

Hitler was a failed house painter and soldier who tried to overthrow the German government in 1923. After serving nine months in jail, he and his Nazi party gained power. The Nazis were anti-Semitic, or prejudiced against Jewish people.

In 1929 the Nazis elected 107 delegates to the Reichstag (the German senate), and four years later German President Paul von Hindenburg gave Adolf Hitler the authority to form a new government.

In 1938, Germany and Austria united, violating a post–World War I treaty; in September that year England's prime minister, Neville Chamberlain, and the heads of France and Italy signed the Munich Agreement with Adolf Hitler. They believed the agreement would keep England from going to war with Germany. They were wrong.

The agreement ceded control of part of Czechoslovakia to Nazi Germany, but Hitler broke the deal after his army seized control of the entire country. Meanwhile, Germany began a massive military buildup. Its men were well trained and well equipped. With their blitzkrieg, or "lightning strike," Nazis had a war machine that was ready for a new battle, another war: World War II.

On September 1, 1939, the German army swept into Poland. Despite having over one million soldiers, the Polish Army was ill equipped and unprepared. The Poles were quickly defeated. Germany and the Union of Soviet Socialist Republics, which included Russia, divided Poland among them.

Prime Minister Chamberlain was forced to declare war, throwing England into the fray. Over the next several years, Germany would invade a number of countries, including France, Holland, and eventually Russia. The war would eventually cost 55 million lives as the Allied Powers of England, France, and Russia were joined by the United States (following the Japan sneak attack on Pearl Harbor in 1941), and the German Axis powers were joined by Italy and Japan.

When he returned to the United States in 1939, Duke confronted Mills, who had a well-deserved reputation for cheating the bands who worked for him. Examining the publisher's financial books, Ellington found a few discrepancies and severed his ties. Signing a three-year agreement with Jack Robbins and the record label Victor, he allowed agency William Morris to handle his concert bookings. Duke felt like he was ready for anything.

In the late 1930s, the Ellington band produced a total of twenty-seven records. One of them included a song called "Something to

Chapter 5 - Summering in Newport

Live For," written by Duke and a man named Billy Strayhorn. Billy was a short man at just five feet three inches, but he had enormous musical talent. He came from Pittsburgh, Pennsylvania, where at the age of nineteen, he heard the Duke Ellington band play at the Stanley Theater. Billy liked the same music that Duke liked and after the concert, he managed to get backstage and play some of his music for Duke. Duke liked what he heard and told Billy to look him up when he got to New York. The following year, Billy went to New York. Duke hired Billy to write songs with him and Billy began to travel with the band. Billy joined Duke about the time he hit his peak and the next several years were highly successful. Duke seemed to turn out one hit after another. Duke and Billy collaborated for almost thirty years.

Billy Strayhorn, shown here with Duke around 1948, was a classically trained composer who collaborated with Duke for nearly thirty years.

As the country suffered through World War II, Duke Ellington and the Washingtonians enjoyed a major triumph. Every performer dreams of playing at Carnegie Hall, New York's premier theater, and in January 1943, Duke and his band began a series of annual concerts, playing there for a dozen years.

In 1945 Allied forces won the war in Europe through conventional means, then used atomic bombs over the Japanese cities of Hiroshima and Nagasaki to gain Japan's formal surrender on August 14, 1945.

Meanwhile, despite the acclaim, Duke's band was getting less and less work. Although his recordings still sold well and he was composing music for movies and television, live bands were falling out of favor. The younger generation seemed to prefer singers like Frank Sinatra and then Elvis Presley.

It took the Newport Jazz Festival to put the band back on the map. Entrepreneur George Wein began the tradition in Newport, Rhode Island, in 1954. Ellington acted as emcee in 1955. The next year he brought the band.

They went on late. It was almost midnight when he started his set with "The Newport Jazz Festival Suite," a song written for the event. With the next song, 1937's "Diminuendo and Crescendo in Blue," the band took off. Drummer Sam Woodyard and bass player Jimmy Woode added a rock beat, and Paul Gonsalves let loose on his saxophone. Before long the audience began to dance. It was so crazy, Wein worried about a riot and yelled to Duke, "That's enough," but Duke kept on playing. He'd afterward say, "I was born in 1956 at the Newport Jazz Festival."[1]

Suddenly the band was hot again and Duke took full advantage. He composed longer works and sacred concerts. Some of his sacred concerts, which focused on Bible scripture, he performed in large churches, such as New York's St. John the Divine and London's Westminster Abbey. He was honored with 13 Grammy Awards and

Chapter 5 - Summering in Newport

16 honorary doctorates from U.S. universities, and the Pulitzer Music committee recommended him for a special prize.

He was still touring constantly when he was diagnosed with lung cancer. He spent his last days at Columbia Presbyterian Medical Center in New York, with a piano in his room. When he had the strength, he would toy with new compositions. He died at the hospital on May 24, 1974.

His son, Mercer Ellington, took over leadership of the band and continued to tour with it for several years. President Richard Nixon said after Duke Ellington's death, "The wit, taste, intelligence and elegance that Duke Ellington brought to his music have made him, in the eyes of millions of people both here and abroad, America's foremost composer. His memory will live for generations to come in the music with which he enriched his nation."[2] ◆

Duke plays guitar and Cab Calloway plays piano during a jam session at a private party hosted by Burris Jenkins (a political cartoonist). The guests included in this picture (left to right) Rosetta Tharpe, Duke Ellington, trumpeter Rex Stewart, and Cab Calloway.

FYInfo

THE POLIO VACCINE

Jonas Salk

Not long before Duke Ellington's rebirth at the Newport Jazz Festival, medical researcher Jonas Salk was enjoying a different kind of triumph.

Since the turn of the 20th century, polio (poliomyelitis) had taken the lives of thousands and crippled millions more. Usually attacking in childhood, the virus became prevalent as cleaner living conditions provided fewer people with the chance to develop an immunity to it. It had even affected a president, Franklin Delano Roosevelt, who would be confined to a wheelchair for the rest of his life after contracting the disease in early adulthood.

In 1927, Roosevelt and his former law partner, Basil O'Connor, established the Warm Springs Foundation, a nonprofit organization aimed at finding a polio cure. Perhaps the first modern organized effort to develop a vaccine, the race to discover a means of preventing polio attracted numerous celebrities who performed in fund-raisers and asked for donations for research. Duke Ellington and his band offered their time and music as researchers raced for a cure. The foundation would eventually become known as the March of Dimes.

Salk's discovery 1954 that a dead strain of the virus was an effective vaccine has saved many lives, and a disease that had crippled many has virtually disappeared.

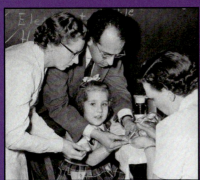

43

Selected Works

1923	"Blind Man's Bluff" (w/ Jo Trent)	1935	"In a Sentimental Mood" (w/ Irving Mills and Manny Kurtz)
1927	"Black and Tan Fantasy" (w/ Bub Miley) "East St. Louis Toodle-Oo"	1937	"Diminuendo and Crescendo in Blue" "Back Room Romp"
1928	"Take It Easy"	1939	"Ko-Ko"
1929	"Big House Blues" "The Mooche" (w/ Irving Mills)	1941	"Take the A Train" (w/ Billy Strayhorn)
1930	"Jazz Lips"	1943	"Savoy Strut" (w/ Johnny Hodges)
1931	"Rockin' in Rhythm" (w/ Irving Mills and Henry Carney) "Dreamy Blues"/"Mood Indigo" (w/ " " and Albert Brigard) "Creole Rhapsody"	1953	"Satin Doll" (w/ Johnny Mercer and Billy Strayhorn)
		1956	"Newport Jazz Festival Suite"
1932	"It Don't Mean a Thing (If It Ain't Got That Swing)" (w/ Irving Mills) "Creole Love Call"	1960	"Black Beauty"
		1962	"Fast and Furious" (w/ Harold Pottio)
1933	"Sophisticated Lady" (w/ Irving Mills and Mitchel Paris)	1966	"Spanking Brand New Doll"
		1970	"Run"
		1973	"Amour, Amour"

Chronology

1899	Born in Washington, D.C., on April 29
1904	Enters Garnet Elementary School
1908	Enters Garrison Public School
1913	Enters Armstrong Manual Training High School to study commercial art
1916	Turns down full scholarship to study art at Pratt Institute in Brooklyn
1917	Drops out of high school three months before graduation; begins playing piano professionally; forms the Duke's Serenaders
1918	Marries Edna Thompson
1919	Son, Mercer Ellington, is born
1923	Moves to New York; forms band, led by Elmer Snowden, first called Elmer Snowden and His Black Sox Orchestra (they are later known as the Washingtonians); the Washingtonians land steady gig at the Hollywood Club (later Club Kentucky)
1924	Snowden leaves the Washingtonians, Ellington becomes leader; Ellington makes first records to be commercially released
1926	Tours New England all summer; meets Irving Mills, who later becomes Ellington's manager
1927	Ellington leads house orchestra at Harlem's Cotton Club, including regular live radio broadcasts
1929	Ellington composes score for and his orchestra appears in RKO motion picture *Black and Tan*; he and Edna separate
1930	Ellington's orchestra appears in *Check and Double Check,* an RKO film starring Amos 'n Andy
1931	Ellington's orchestra leaves Cotton Club, begins touring
1932	Records "It Don't Mean a Thing (If It Ain't Got That Swing)"
1933	First European tour
1935	Mother, Daisy Ellington, dies

Chronology (cont'd)

- 1937   CBS Radio begins *Saturday Night Swing Session*—Ellington is featured three times; J.E. Ellington, his father, dies
- 1938   Ellington breaks from Irving Mills, signs with William Morris Agency; begins 29-year collaboration with Billy Strayhorn
- 1939   Second European tour; new recording contract with Victor
- 1943   Begins annual concerts at Carnegie Hall
- 1956   Appears at Newport Jazz Festival
- 1959   Composes sound track for *Anatomy of a Murder*
- 1965   Recommended for Special Award by the Pulitzer Music Committee
- 1966   Is presented with the President's Gold Medal on behalf of Lyndon Johnson
- 1969   Richard Nixon presents Ellington with the Presidential Medal of Freedom
- 1973   Publishes *Music Is My Mistress*
- 1974   Dies of lung cancer on May 24; Western High School in Washington, D.C., is renamed Duke Ellington School for the Arts
- 1976   Pop singer and composer Stevie Wonder releases his hit "Sir Duke," which honors Duke Ellington and other music pioneers
- 1986   U.S. Postal Service issues Duke Ellington commemorative stamp
- 1987   His archive is preserved at the Smithsonian Institution
- 2000   Posthumously wins his 12th and 13th Grammy Awards for *The Duke Ellington Centennial Edition—The Complete RCA Victor Recordings (1927–1973)* (Best Historical Album) and *Bennett Sings Ellington—Hot and Cool* (Traditional Pop Vocal Performance, by Tony Bennett)

Timeline in History

- 1896   The U.S. Supreme Court rules in *Plessy v. Ferguson* that "separate but equal" facilities for blacks and whites is constitutional.
- 1901   Educator Booker T. Washington becomes the first African American to be served dinner in the White House; Guglielmo Marconi sends radio signals across the English Channel.
- 1914   The Panama Canal, a passage through Central America connecting the Atlantic and Pacific Oceans, is opened.
- 1917   The U.S. joins World War I; the war will end the next year.
- 1919   Race riots explode in 19 U.S. cities.
- 1920   Prohibition becomes the law across the United States; it is repealed in 1933.
- 1923   The Harlem Renaissance begins.
- 1927   *The Jazz Singer* is the first movie with a sound track. Charles Lindbergh makes first solo flight across the Atlantic.
- 1929   A stock market crash leads to the Great Depression.
- 1941   The United States enters World War II.
- 1943   Race riots again explode in Harlem and many other cities.
- 1945   World War II ends.
- 1948   Television sets become common in U.S. households.
- 1954   The U.S. Supreme Court bans school segregation.
- 1955   Martin Luther King Jr. launches Montgomery bus boycott after Rosa Parks is arrested for sitting in the white section of a city bus.
- 1963   U.S. President John F. Kennedy is assassinated.
- 1974   President Richard Nixon resigns.
- 1999   Worldwide celebration of the centennial of Duke Ellington's birth.

Chapter Notes

Chapter 1   The Piano, Man
1. John Edward Hasse, *Beyond Category: The Life and Genius of Duke Ellington* (New York: Simon & Schuster, 1993), p. 36.

Chapter 2   A Royal Childhood
1. Edward Kennedy Ellington, *Music Is My Mistress* (New York: Doubleday, 1973; Da Capo Press, 1988), p.43.
2. John Edward Hasse, *Beyond Category: The Life and Genius of Duke Ellington* (New York: Simon & Schuster, 1993), p. 24.
3. Edward Kennedy Ellington, *Music Is My Mistress* (New York: Doubleday, 1973; Da Capo Press, 1988), p.66.

Chapter 3   Leader of the Band
1. John Edward Hasse, *Beyond Category: The Life and Genius of Duke Ellington* (New York: Simon & Schuster, 1993), p. 45.
2. Ibid., p. 53
3. Cab Calloway and Bryant Rollins, *Of Minnie the Moocher and Me* (New York: Thomas Y. Crowell, 1976), p. 88.

Chapter 4   Duke of Harlem
1. Mark Tucker, *The Duke Ellington Reader* (New York: Oxford University Press, 1993), p. 22.
2. John Edward Hasse, *Beyond Category: The Life and Genius of Duke Ellington* (New York: Simon & Schuster, 1993), p. 112.
3. Ibid., p. 196.

Chapter 5   Summering in Newport
1. John Edward Hasse, *Beyond Category: The Life and Genius of Duke Ellington* (New York: Simon & Schuster, 1993), p. 322.
2. Historic U Street Jazz, "Ellington's Washington," (http://www.gwu.edu/-jazz/performersd.html).

For Further Reading

For Young Adults
Brown, Gene. *Duke Ellington: Jazz Master.* Giants of Art and Culture. San Diego: Blackbirch Press, 2001.
Terrill, Richard. *Duke Ellington.* African-American Biographies. Austin, Tex.: Raintree-Steck Vaughn, 2003.
Traus, Dempsey J. *The Duke Ellington Primer.* Chicago: Urban Research Press, Inc., 1996.

Internet Addresses
Amazing Americans: Duke Ellington
    http://www.americaslibrary.gov/cgi-bin/page.cgi/aa/ellington
Duke Ellington
    http://www.galegroup.com/free_resources/bhm/bio/ellington_d.htm
Duke Ellington –Celebrating 100 Years of the Man and His Music
    http://dellington.org

For Further Reading (cont'd)

Duke Ellington Centennial Celebration, National Museum of American History
   http://americanhistory.si.edu/events/elling/index.htm
Duke Ellington Collection Tour, National Museum of American History
   http://americanhistory.si.edu/archives/de-tour/ppreview.htm
Duke Ellington—Official Site
   http://www.dukeellington.com/
Duke Ellington's Washington
   http://www.pbs.org/ellingtonsdc/
Duke Ellington's Washington: The Music Scene
   http://www.pbs.org/ellingtonsdc/musicScene.htm
Edward "Duke" Ellington, 1899–1974
   http://www.redhotjazz.com/duke.html
Edward K. "Duke" Ellington.
   http://www.schirmer.com/composers/ellington_bio.html
Harlem 1900–1940: Edward Kennedy "Duke" Ellington
   http://www.si.umich.edu/CHICO/Harlem/text/ellington.html
Historic U Street Jazz, "Ellington's Washington," http://www.gwu.edu/-jazz/
   performersd.html

Works Consulted

Calloway, Cab, and Bryant Rollins. *Of Minnie the Moocher and Me.* New York: Thomas Y. Crowell, 1976.
Collier, James Lincoln. *Duke Ellington.* New York: Macmillan, 1991.
Ellington, Duke. *Ken Burns Jazz—Duke Ellington* (CD). New York: Sony Music, 2000.
Ellington, Edward Kennedy. *Music Is My Mistress.* New York: Doubleday, 1973; Da Capo Press, 1988.
Gaines, Patrice. "Ellington, the Duke of Musical Royalty." *The Washington Post,* April 29, 1989. Reprinted at http://www.washingtonpost.com/wp-srv/style/music/features/ellington/tribute.htm.
Hasse, John Edward. *Beyond Category: The Life and Genius of Duke Ellington.* New York: Simon & Schuster, 1993.
Nicholson, Stuart. *Reminiscing in Tempo: A Portrait of Duke Ellington.* Boston: Northern University Press, 1999.
Tucker, Mark. *Ellington: The Early Years.* Urbana, Ill.: University of Illinois, 1991.
———. *The Duke Ellington Reader.* New York: Oxford University Press, 1993.

Sidebars

"Records and Radios"
   "The Invention of the Radio"
   www.alpcom.it/hamradio/radeng.html
"The Summer of Fear"
   http://www.lib.uchicago.edu/ecuip/diglib/social/chi1919/aline/a2/precop.html
"Langston Hughes: The Renaissance Reporter"
   "Meet Amazing Americans: Langston Hughes"
   http://www.americaslibrary.gov/cgi-bin/page.cgi/aa/hughes
"'That Swing'"
   "History of Swing Dancing"
   www.centralhome.com/ballroomcountry/swing.htm
"The Polio Vaccine"
   "The March of Dimes Story: Uniting to Beat Polio"
   http://www.marchofdimes.com/aboutus/789_821.asp

Index

Armstrong, Louis 33
Brooks, Harvey 7, 15, 16
Calloway, Cab 22, 23
Cotton Club 31, 36
Dorsey, Jimmy 37
Edison, Thomas 9, 11
Ellington, Daisy (mother) 13
Ellington, Edward Kennedy (Duke)
    birth of 12
    diagnosed with lung cancer 42
    education 14-15
    European tour (1939) 38
    father dies 37
    forms Duke's Serenaders 20
    hears Harvey Brooks play 7
    marries 21
    mother dies 37
    plays at Hollywood Club (Club Kentucky) 28, 29, 30
    sister 16
    son is born 21
Ellington, James Edward (father) 13
Ellington, Mercer (son) 21
Fitzgerald, F. Scott 21
Goodman, Benny 37
Greer, William 23, 24, 27
Hardwick, Otto 24
Harlem 22, 23
Hitler, Adolf 38
Hughes, Langston 22, 25
Lindbergh, Charles 33
Marconi, Guglielmo 9
McEntree, Edward 15
Mills, Irving 30, 35, 36, 39
Morris, William 39
Newport Jazz Festival 41
Prohibition 21
Robbins, Jack 39
Salk, Jonas 43
Sandburg, Carl 17
Schribman, Charles 29
Snowden, Elmer 28
Sousa, John Philip 12
Speakeasies 21, 35
Stewart, Rex 22
stock market crash (1929) 31
Strayhorn, Billy 40
Sweatman, Wilbur 23, 24
Thompson, Edna (wife) 20, 21
Trent, Jo 27, 29
World War I 19, 21, 22
World War II 39